ANIMALS UNDER THE
GRAY WOLF

IN DANGER OF EXTINCTION!

Jill Bailey

Heinemann Library
Chicago, Illinois

P9-BXZ-727

© 2005 Heinemann Library
a division of Reed Elsevier Inc.
Chicago, Illinois

Customer Service   888–454–2279

Visit our website at www.heinemannlibrary.com

All rights reserved. No part of this publication may be reproduced or transmitted in any form or by any means, electronic or mechanical, including photocopying, recording, taping, or any information storage and retrieval system, without permission in writing from the publisher.

Photo research by Laura Durman
Designed by Ian Winton and Jo Malivoire
Printed in China by WKT Company Limited

09 08 07 06 05
10 9 8 7 6 5 4 3 2 1

Library of Congress Cataloging-in-Publication Data
Bailey, Jill.
  Gray wolf / Jill Bailey.
      p. cm. — (Animals under threat)
  Includes bibliographical references (p.   ) and index.
  ISBN 1-4034-5583-X (hardcover) — ISBN 1-4034-5690-9 (pbk.)
  1. Wolves—Juvenile literature. I. Title. II. Series.
  QL737.C22B334 2004
  599.773—dc22
                                    2004000566

Acknowledgments
The author and publisher are grateful to the following for permission to reproduce copyright material: Ardea pp. **8** (Bill Coster/Ardea London), **40** (Mary Clay/Ardea London); Bruce Coleman Collection pp. **12** (Hans Reinhard), **13** (Bruce Coleman Inc.), **39** (Werner Layer); Corbis pp. **14** (Royalty-Free/Corbis), **23** (Peter Turnley), **25**, **26** (Hulton-Deutsch Collection), **28** (Bettmann), **29** (Layne Kennedy), **31** (Layne Kennedy), **32** (Lynda Richardson), **34** (Campbell William/Corbis Sygma); Frank Lane Picture Agency pp. **7** (S. Yoshino/Minden Pictures), **16** (A. Bardi/Panda Photo), **27** (G. Marcoaldi/Panda Photo), **41** (N. Biet/Panda Photo); Getty Images pp. **11**, **17** (both by Jim and Jamie Dutcher); International Wolf Centre (www.wolf.org) pp. **19** (Lynn and Donna Rogers - www.bearstudy.org), **33** (USFWS and Barron Crawford), **35**, **42**, **43**; Mary Evans Picture Library pp. **20**, **24**; NHPA pp. **5** (T. Kitchin and V. Hurst); Rolf O. Peterson pp. **30**, **37**; Still Pictures pp. **4** (Klein/Hubert), **36** (William Campbell), **38** (Peter Weimann); Team Husar.com pp. **10**, **18** (both by Lisa and Mike Husar). Header image reproduced with permission of PhotoDisc.

Cover photograph reproduced with permission of NHPA/David Middleton.

Every effort has been made to contact copyright holders of any material reproduced in this book. Any omissions will be rectified in subsequent printings if notice is given to the publisher.

Some words are shown in bold, **like this.** You can find out what they mean by looking in the glossary.

Contents

The Wild Wolf

The gray wolf is the largest member of the dog family. Many people are afraid of wolves. Others admire them as a symbol of the wilderness. The gray wolf is a remarkable animal. It is able to survive in some of the least hospitable places on Earth. Despite its fierce, even savage, reputation the gray wolf is a devoted parent. Wolf relatives share the care of the young, and help older or weaker members of their group.

The gray wolf is a **predator.** It lives by hunting and eating other animals (prey). The prey ranges from large animals, such as moose, bison (buffalo), and deer to smaller creatures, such as hares, beavers, and even mice. The type of prey available depends on the time of year and where the wolf lives. While some wolves live alone, most live in packs (groups). A pack of wolves can bring down prey as large as a bison, an animal ten times the weight of a single wolf. On some occasions, even a lone wolf may successfully kill a deer.

Admired and hated!

Native Americans admire the wolf for its courage, cunning, and survival skills. Many of their rituals have grown up using wolf symbols or skins. To them it is a natural part of the wilderness. On the other hand, most **ranchers** and reindeer herders hate the wolf because it kills their livestock and costs them money. Hunters see the wolf as a competitor to be eliminated. Farmers turn the wolf's habitat into fields, and cities and roads cover the wilderness in concrete.

A wolf is the size of a large dog. It is up to 31 inches (81 centimeters) at the shoulder and 6.5 feet (2 meters) from the nose to the tip of its tail.

Wolves live and hunt in packs. Most members of the pack belong to the same family. This pack is sharing a kill.

A top dog

Gray wolves have few natural enemies. Their main enemy is humans. In some **habitats,** such as the northern forests of North America, they have tough competitors, like the brown bear. The brown bear can drive wolves off their kills and force them to spend more time hunting. However, no animals deliberately hunt down and kill adult wolves.

In truly wild places, wolves can help to control the populations of their prey. Deer and moose populations tend to vary dramatically. When food is plentiful, and there are few or no predators, the populations increase rapidly. The plants they eat are unable to grow back fast enough, so the animals start to run out of food. The population then crashes. Wolves tend to attack mainly sick and old animals, and the very young. This slows the rate of growth of the prey population, and helps to prevent diseases from spreading. By removing weak individuals so that they do not breed, wolves help to maintain a healthy stock of prey.

Wolves Worldwide

The wolf is one of the most widely distributed large **predators** in the world. It once roamed the entire northern hemisphere from the Arctic Ocean to Mexico. It was found in the Mediterranean, Arabia, India, and Japan, in almost every **habitat.** The main prey of most wolves are large, hoofed, grazing mammals (ungulates), such as moose, elk, reindeer (caribou), bison, and antelopes. In order to find enough food, wolves must live in large, unspoiled, wilderness areas, such as forests, mountains, grasslands, and the **tundra.**

If human settlements come close to wolf territory, wolves also eat domestic livestock—for example, sheep, goats, cattle, and even horses—as well as cats and dogs. The gradual spread of humans across the globe has brought people and their animals into conflict with wolves. It has also led to competition between humans and wolves to hunt animals, such as deer.

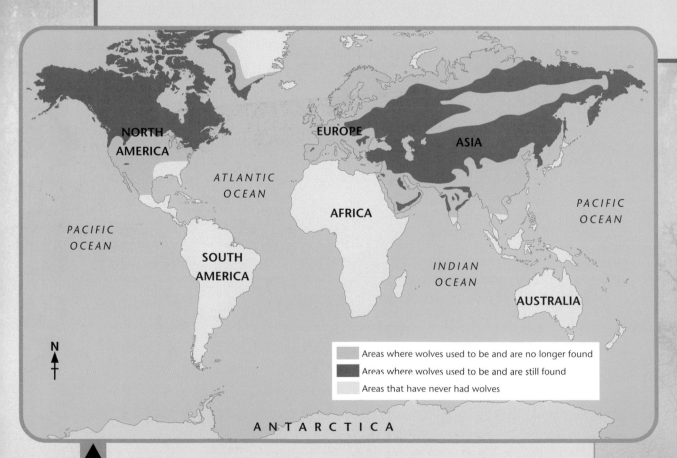

Areas where wolves used to be and are no longer found
Areas where wolves used to be and are still found
Areas that have never had wolves

This map shows the distribution of the gray wolf across the world today (in red) and in earlier times (in green). What it does not show is that while wolves may still survive in some places today, there are far fewer of them than there used to be.

Once there were vast areas of North America with millions of bison, supporting thousands of wolves, but now scenes like this are a rare sight—the wolves and their prey have largely disappeared.

Wolves at war

Over the centuries, humans moved in on the wolf's natural habitat. The loss of habitat and prey made the wolves more likely to turn to sheep and cattle for food. Farmers, hunters, and governments have hunted the wolf. This has drastically reduced wolf numbers to the point where they have disappeared from large areas, and become **extinct** in some countries. In others there remain only scattered lone wolves or pairs.

There are now very few wild wolves in Germany and France. The last wolves in the United Kingdom were hunted to extinction in Scotland in the middle of the 1600s. In the United States, many states no longer have wolves. In densely populated parts of Asia, such as India, wolves are declining fast as their habitat disappears, and conflicts with expanding human populations become more frequent. In Scandinavia, numbers are so low that packs are rare, and many wolves live alone or in pairs.

Fighting for territory

A wolf pack defends an area of land large enough to provide sufficient prey to support the pack and its offspring. This is called its territory. Usually a pack advertises its territory by means of scent marks and howling, so other wolves know to keep their distance. However, where wolf populations are expanding or where prey becomes scarce, encounters with neighbors are more frequent. The competing wolves become highly aggressive and fights often prove deadly. In the absence of humans, injuries from fights are the biggest cause of death among wolves.

The gray wolf has a long history, dating back perhaps a million years. It is a **species,** which means that it is unlikely to breed with other kinds of wolves. Every species has a unique two-part Latin name—a **genus** name and a species name. The gray wolf belongs to the genus *Canis* that also includes domestic dogs, jackals, and coyotes. The gray wolf is *Canis lupus*.

Over long periods of time, populations on different continents, or separated by large areas with no suitable **habitat,** gradually change. Those animals best suited to local conditions are more likely to survive and produce young. Eventually a population changes so much that it can no longer interbreed with other populations—it has become a new species. However, before it reaches this stage, it is known as a **subspecies.**

Wolf subspecies

There are about 11 subspecies of the gray wolf. They range from the large, heavy Alaskan/Canadian wolf, to the small Arabian wolf. The gray wolf is believed to have developed in Asia, from animal ancestors that **migrated** there from North America between 1 and 2 million years ago. It spread west to Europe, and probably crossed into North America about 300,000 years ago, when there was an ice bridge across the Bering Sea between Asia and North America.

A pack of coyotes surveys a flock of snow geese in New Mexico. Many coyotes live alone, but some live and hunt in packs.

Mixed-up species

Coyotes, or **prairie** wolves (*Canis latrans*), were already in North America when the gray wolf arrived, as was another wolf, the dire wolf (*Canis dirus*). Coyotes, gray, and dire wolves are all probably descended from a common ancestor. The coyote looks like a cross between a small wolf and a fox. On occasions, the gray wolf and coyote may interbreed, forming **hybrids.**

The mysterious red wolf

Scientists cannot decide whether the red wolf is a subspecies of the gray wolf, a species in its own right (*Canis rufus*), or a hybrid between the gray wolf and the coyote. Once common in the southeastern United States, it was hunted almost to extinction. There are probably very few pure red wolves today, other than a few in captivity. **Genetic** evidence suggests that it may have been a separate species long ago, but has interbred with coyotes and gray wolves for thousands of years. The distinction is important. If it is not a species, it is not protected by **conservation legislation.**

The dire wolf (now **extinct**) was a scavenger. It was the size of a large gray wolf, but had a broader head and shorter, sturdier legs. Its massive teeth were **adapted** for crushing bone. It could not run very fast, and it probably lived like a hyena, feeding mainly on carcasses. It is believed to have fed on the remains of enormous grazing mammals, such as mammoths, and very large relatives of horses and deer. About 10,000 years ago, at the end of the last Ice Age, these large grazers disappeared, and with them the dire wolf.

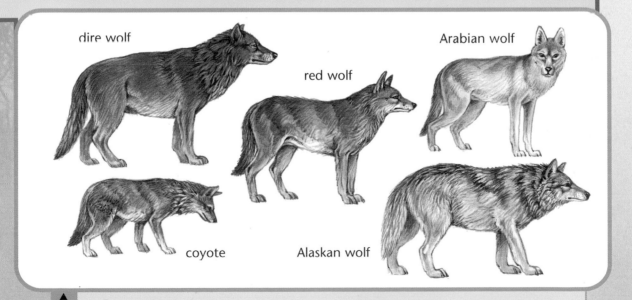

This illustration shows some of the different subspecies and hybrids of the gray wolf. The dire wolf is now extinct.

The Wolf Pack

The wolf pack is usually an extended family group. This generally consists of a breeding pair, their offspring, and other nonbreeding adults. Each wolf has its own rank within the pack, superior to some members and inferior to others. The breeding pair—the **alpha** male and female—is at the top of the pack and young or weaker wolves are at the bottom. Individuals vary greatly in size, physical strength, and personality.

Dominant wolves are naturally bolder than lower-ranking animals, who may get bullied by the others. Wolves are highly competitive animals, and become aggressive when challenged. However, they have developed an elaborate system of body positions, facial expressions, and sounds that allow them to judge each other without fighting.

These wolves are greeting the leader of the pack. The one on its back is giving a submissive display, to show the leader it respects his authority.

Territory

A wolf pack usually hunts over a particular area, called its territory. It defends this territory against other wolves, attacking them if they come across its borders. By doing so, the pack ensures it has a big enough area over which to hunt to feed its members and their pups. The size of the territory depends on the size of the pack and the amount of available prey. The largest wolf pack on record contained 42 animals, but packs are usually much smaller than this. If there is plenty of prey available all year, a territory as small as 13 square miles (33 square kilometers) may be enough to support a small pack.

The alpha wolf threatens to bite the nose of a subordinate wolf, to demonstrate its authority.

If there is less prey, a wolf pack may travel large distances. The largest territory on record is several thousand square miles. In this case, the wolves lived in different parts of the territory at different times of the year. Wolves that follow **migrating** reindeer or antelope may cover an area greater than over 38,000 square miles (100,000 square kilometers) during one year. This is not a true territory, however, because the wolves do not actively defend the whole migration route.

Splitting up

If there are too many wolves in relation to the amount of food, some may break away and form new packs elsewhere. If the wolves did not leave, the pack would have to defend a large territory, and would spend too much time and energy traveling in search of prey. Neighboring packs, especially those that are closely related, may join together in good times and separate again when food becomes scarce.

Lone wolves

A wolf is quite capable of surviving on its own. Many young wolves leave their family group to seek a mate and start a new pack or, on rare occasions, to join another pack. They can travel up to 500 miles (800 kilometers) in search of unoccupied territory. Older, low-ranking wolves may be driven from a pack by bullying. In Norway and Sweden, where there are very few wolves left, most live alone or in pairs. Lone wolves are also common in parts of the Middle East, where road kill and livestock carcasses provide easily accessible food.

Body of a Hunter

The gray wolf's body is built for roaming and hunting over distance. Its long legs give it a loping stride. Like other dogs, the wolf walks on its toes rather than on the pads of its feet. This reduces friction and makes long-distance travel less tiring. The wolf's blunt claws enable it to grip and move easily over rocky ground. Wolves can run at speeds of 40 miles per hour (64 kilometers per hour) but they cannot keep this up for long. They are best at loping along for mile after mile, covering up to 45 miles (72 kilometers) a day, at an average speed of about 5 miles per hour (8 kilometers per hour). They can also swim distances of up to 8 miles (13 kilometers), aided by small webs between their toes.

Large and powerful

An average male wolf is almost as long as a human is tall. It stands between 5 and 7 feet (1.5 to 2 meters) from nose to tail tip, and between 26 and 32 inches (66 to 81 centimeters) in height at the shoulder. The female wolf is smaller. Desert wolves tend to be smaller than average, while the **tundra** wolves are the largest. They are powerful enough to bring down a large deer. A wolf may live for 13 years in the wild, and up to 17 years in captivity.

How to tell the age of a wolf

During its life, the wolf's tough diet of meat, skin, and bones steadily wears down its teeth. By the time it reaches old age, the wolf's long, pointed, canine teeth may be half their original length, while its incisors may be worn right down to the roots. The enamel on the wolf's teeth grows thinner with age and the gums recede, exposing the base of each tooth. Scientists can therefore tell the age of a wolf by looking at its teeth.

A wolf is built for long-distance travel. It can guard a large area to get enough food for its family.

Wolves have a powerful sense of smell and good hearing. They can detect sounds of higher pitch than humans can hear. Their eyes are particularly good at detecting movement.

The wolf captures and kills its prey with its teeth. It has a long skull with large jaws worked by powerful muscles, and its bite packs a pressure of nearly 1,500 pounds per square inch (105 kilograms per square centimeter). The long, fang-like canine teeth near the front of the jaw help the wolf grip its prey and rip into flesh, and powerful, sharp-edged teeth called carnassials cut flesh from bones. The teeth at the back of the mouth crack and crush bones. The smaller front teeth (incisors) stick out beyond the canines, so they can be used to grip and pull at the flesh of both live and dead prey.

Coat color

The term *gray wolf* is rather misleading. Gray wolves may be gray, black, cream, or even pure white; some have beige or reddish coats. Pale wolves are most common in Arctic regions. Most wolves are a sort of spotted gray, but a single litter may contain pups of various colors. Like humans, wolves tend to become grayer with age.

Pack Power

The secret of the gray wolf's wide distribution and its survival against the odds is its **adaptability.** As well as having an astonishing sense of smell, the wolf can also detect sounds up to 10 miles (16 kilometers) away. These qualities, together with the ability to see at night, mean that it can hunt around the clock. Working in a pack, wolves are capable of bringing down prey, such as bison, moose, and musk oxen. These animals are 10 times the size of an individual wolf. Wolves can also survive on a diet of mice and carrion (dead flesh). A wolf may eat 20 pounds (9 kilograms) of meat at a single sitting, then go for weeks without eating.

Wolves take advantage of the seasons. They hunt calves and fawns (young deer) in spring, male moose, male bison, and stags (male deer) in the fall (when the males are weakened by the **rut**), and old and very young animals in the winter, when the prey is weakened by cold and lack of food. Wolves have also been known to fish for salmon. They wade in and herd the fish into shallow pools, where the fish are trapped and easy to catch. Alternatively, a wolf may hunt from the riverbank, plunging its long, narrow snout in to grab the fish.

▲ A particularly large pack of wolves sets out to hunt on a snowy Italian mountainside.

Wolf and prey

A pack of wolves disturbs a large moose, which takes to its heels. The wolves chase it. The moose stops and turns to face them. The wolves pull up and keep their distance, watchful and wary—eventually they move away. Even smaller prey may be left alone if they stand their ground. Sick animals often make no attempt to flee or defend themselves. They provide an easy source of food for wolves.

A wolf pack gathers for the hunt. The wolves' large paws help them stay on top of the snow, but deep snow can weaken prey animals such as deer as they try to wade through it.

Hunting strategy

Wolves capture small prey easily by stalking and pouncing, but hunting large prey is dangerous. Wolves can die or get seriously maimed as a result of a kick from an elk or moose, or by a thrust of its antlers. Wolves use teamwork to distract the prey. Some attack its **flanks** while others seize its head and neck, biting and clinging, even dangling from it. A common tactic is to seize the nose until the prey starts to suffocate and sinks to its knees. Even weak members of the pack play a part. Old wolves may have expert tracking skills and a good memory of the territory.

The secret of the wolf's hunting ability is its stamina. A wolf can pursue prey relentlessly, sometimes for hours, until the victim gets tired. Wolves usually stalk their prey for many miles, assessing them, looking for weaklings and stragglers. Often they pretend to attack, then withdraw. This tests the prey's readiness to fight back or flee. Repeated challenges may force the prey to flee, revealing the slow and weak. Wolves chase far more animals than they actually attack. Even when they do attack, they only kill about one in ten victims.

Bringing Up the Young

In most wolf packs, only the **alpha** male and female breed. They prevent others from breeding by threats and bullying. If there is a lot of prey, a second pair may be allowed to breed. In this way wolves regulate the size of the pack so that it does not run out of food.

The female wolf mates only once a year, for five to fourteen days . This happens between late January and early March or April. Her pregnancy lasts for about nine weeks. There is a lot more aggression around mating time. The wolves seek to establish and maintain their rank in the pack. Young and low-ranking wolves often grow tired of being bullied and being the last to eat. They sometimes decide to leave the pack.

These cubs are snuggling up for warmth and safety. The wolf cubs will feed on their mother's milk for at least five weeks. The pack stays nearby to protect the female and her cubs.

A family affair

All the wolves help dig a den in which the female gives birth. This is usually a hole in the ground, but a hollow log or cave can be used instead. The young are born in spring, when the prey animals also give birth, and food is plentiful. While the pups are very tiny, the pack stays in the area around the den. Wolf pups are born helpless, blind, and deaf. They rely on their mother's milk until they are about five weeks old. Then they are fed on half-digested meat spit up by the adults. Most members of the pack help to guard and feed the young. At about one month old, the pups emerge from the den and start to

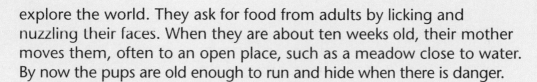

explore the world. They ask for food from adults by licking and nuzzling their faces. When they are about ten weeks old, their mother moves them, often to an open place, such as a meadow close to water. By now the pups are old enough to run and hide when there is danger.

Moving on

At about four months old, the pups are strong enough to accompany the adults to kills. In the fall, they start to follow the hunt. They put into practice the skills they began to learn through play. Now the pack can move on to other places in its territory. At one year old, the young are fully grown. They may stay in the pack for up to three more years, improving their hunting skills and helping to care for new brothers and sisters. They may leave the pack to find a mate and start a pack of their own.

The importance of play

Pups love to play. They stalk, chase, pounce, and paw at each other. But this is not just play—they will need these skills for the hunt later in their lives. Through play they learn the gestures vital for socializing with other wolves—bows, tail wags, and aggressive and submissive postures. In games like tag, keep away, wrestling, and king of the hill, they learn to interact with other wolves and develop long-lasting social bonds. The exercise also helps their muscles to grow and improves their coordination.

Play is an important part of growing up, helping to build the strong muscles and quick responses that will be needed in the hunt.

Although a wolf may live for up to thirteen years, many never reach that age. Before they become old enough to suffer the diseases of old age, such as cancer, **arthritis,** heart disease, and kidney disease, most wolves will die. Many wolves are injured or killed by hunters and farmers. Traps and snares set for other animals can also capture and injure a wolf, who may even bite off a foot to escape. Some die from injuries they received during the hunt or in fights with other wolves. Young wolves learning to hunt are particularly at risk, because they are weak and inexperienced at steering clear of horns and hooves.

Adult wolves are remarkably tough. They can survive broken ribs from the kick of a deer, and even skull fractures and broken legs. Sometimes, however, wounds become infected, and **gangrene** may set in. Wolves with limb deformities are less able to hunt and, unless the pack supports them, they become weakened by hunger and susceptible to disease. Older wolves often suffer arthritis in damaged joints.

This picture shows an Italian woman snatching her child away from the jaws of a large wolf. When wolves are suffering from rabies, they may attack and bite humans. Such attacks are very rare.

Rabies

For centuries, humans have had a great fear of wolf attacks, and the wolf has been hated as a result. Tales of attacks increased the wolf's fearful reputation. Most fatal attacks are made by wolves or wolf-dog **hybrids** suffering from rabies. This virus affects the brain. Wolves with rabies produce lots of saliva, and bite other animals and even lifeless objects. Rabies is passed in the saliva of bites. It can be passed from dogs and wolves to humans, and is often deadly.

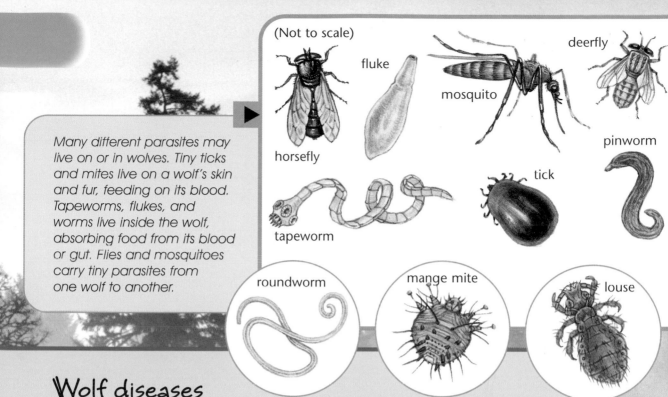

(Not to scale)

fluke

deerfly

mosquito

horsefly

pinworm

tick

tapeworm

roundworm

mange mite

louse

Many different parasites may live on or in wolves. Tiny ticks and mites live on a wolf's skin and fur, feeding on its blood. Tapeworms, flukes, and worms live inside the wolf, absorbing food from its blood or gut. Flies and mosquitoes carry tiny parasites from one wolf to another.

Wolf diseases

Many of the diseases caused by viruses and bacteria that affect domestic dogs are also a danger to wolves. Such diseases include rabies **distemper,** and **canine parvovirus.** In the wild, contact with other wolf packs is limited, but as more humans move to wilderness areas or visit them for recreation, wolves come into increased contact with domestic dogs and are at risk of picking up infections that they have no natural resistance to.

Parasites

Many tiny animals live on and inside wolves. Parasites, such as lice, fleas, ticks, and mites hide in their fur and feed on their blood and tissues. If there are a lot of parasites, the wolf may become tired, or may be so distracted by itching and scratching that it does not catch enough prey. **Mange** mites can cause the wolf to lose much of its fur, making it susceptible to the cold and to other skin infections. Other external insects, such as deerflies, horseflies, blackflies, and mosquitoes, steal a quick meal of blood and move away, but their saliva may transmit viruses and other diseases.

Inside the wolf is another assortment of unwanted creatures— tapeworms, roundworms, **hookworms,** and **flukes.** Tapeworms and roundworms live in the wolf's intestine, absorbing already digested food through their skins. They release millions of tiny eggs that pass out in the wolf's droppings, to be picked up by other animals. Wolves become infected when they eat one of these animals. A heavy load of internal parasites can make a wolf more susceptible to diseases.

Wolves and Humans

The earliest drawings of wolves are in caves in southern Europe, and date from 20,000 B.C.E. In those days, humans lived in small communities much like wolves, sheltering in caves and hunting grazing mammals. There was plenty of prey, so wolves had no reason to attack humans, and humans had no reason to attack wolves.

Some time around 5,000 B.C.E. or even earlier, humans began to develop agriculture and herd livestock. From this point on, everything changed. Wolves were deprived of their natural **habitat** and prey by human farming methods and forest clearing. They therefore began to attack livestock which, after all, looked very much like their natural prey.

Attacks on humans—fact or fiction?

Most of the time wolves avoid humans, slipping quietly away when they approach. Unless a pack of wolves is starving, a single shepherd can usually drive it off. Humans are not the wolf's natural prey. However, fear of wolf attacks increased dramatically in Europe as the human population grew and moved into wolf territory. Until about 200 years ago, rabies was common in Europe. A **rabid** wolf will attack humans—and any other animal. But far more common are attacks by large dogs and the wolf-dog **hybrids** that are often mistaken for true wolves. In the last 50 years, no one has been killed by wolves in North America. Only seven people in all of Europe have been killed.

Long ago humans lived in small groups and hunted their prey alongside wolves. In the picture below, humans and wolves are hunting bison.

Some Native Americans used to cover themselves in wolf skins as a disguise to get close to animals they were hunting. This ceremonial Comanche outfit includes a wolf skin headdress.

Spirit power

Some cultures, such as the Nunamiut Inupiat of Alaska and the Celts and Anglo-Saxons of Britain, continued to see wolves as a natural part of their environment. They admired the wolves' skill in hunting, and human hunters and heroes often took wolf names such as Rudolf (from *Ruhm-wolf*, meaning "victorious wolf" in the Norse language). Hunting and healing rituals developed involving wolves, wolf skins, and wolf bones.

Wolves were thought to have spiritual and healing powers. The Alaskan Tanaina believed wolves were once people, and saw them as family members. The Japanese word for *wolf* means "great god." Until the 1800s, Japanese people saw wolves as allies. Wolves killed the deer and other animals that damaged and ate people's crops.

Legend claims that a female wolf brought up the twins Romulus and Remus, the founders of Rome. Other tales of humans brought up by wolves are surprisingly common in Europe. Some may be based in fact. Small children have wandered off and been found in a wolf's den. There are a few authentic records of wolves allowing tiny children to mingle with their pups without harming them.

An Unreasonable Fear

While hunters may have respected and admired the wolf, **nomads,** who wandered the wilderness with their flocks of sheep and goats, saw the wolf as an enemy. The Greek storyteller Aesop, who lived in the 6th century B.C.E., wrote fables describing the cunning and deceit of the wolf.

Enemy of the gods

According to legend, the Greek god Apollo took on the form of a wolf to fight, but he was also known as the wolf slayer. In **Nordic** legends, Odin, ruler of the gods, always had two wolves beside him. It was said that the end of the world would come when Skoll and his brother Hati, two giants disguised as wolves, finally devoured the Sun and the Moon. At this time the giant wolf, Fenris, would be set loose to attack and kill Odin and the gods.

In this early 20th-century illustration, a werewolf returns home from a night hunting.

Werewolves

For hundreds of years, there have been stories of werewolves—people who were said to turn into wolves at night, often at certain stages of the moon. This fear became widespread in the Middle Ages, and persists in remote parts of Russia to this day. Werewolves were said to have made a pact with the devil, or to have been turned into werewolves as a punishment for sinning. Churches had great power in the Middle Ages, and great influence on the laws of the land. Some church leaders denounced werewolves in church. They put pressure on local lawmakers to criminalize them. Many people were executed for a crime called lycanthropy (being werewolves). Today there are still movies and books written about werewolves.

▲ *This is an illustration from* Red Riding Hood, *one of the many fairy tales where a wolf is the villain.*

Pact with the devil

In the Middle Ages (500 to 1500 C.E.), the wolf was feared as an enemy of humans. Ancient associations of the wolf with the supernatural increased people's fears. Many traditional children's tales, such as *Red Riding Hood* and *The Three Little Pigs,* have a wolf as the villain.

Times were hard, and people looked for something to take out their frustrations on. Governments ordered wolf hunts, sometimes compelling thousands of people to take part. Packs of starving stray dogs were common at the time, and so was rabies. Unprovoked attacks by large **rabid** dogs were often attributed to wolves, further fueling people's fears.

Humans have used every means at their disposal to kill wolves. In India, simple pit traps are used, disguised with branches or leaves. The wolves fall in and people then stone them to death. Early hunters used bows and arrows, then guns. A common method was to wait for parents to leave the pups, then raid the den, kill the pups, and shoot the parents as they returned.

▲ A hunter returns to a leg trap to find a dead wolf caught by its paw. Such traps catch many other animals indiscriminately, and could seriously injure humans, too.

Trappers who wanted to sell wolf skins did not want bullet holes in them, so they used steel leg-hold traps. These traps do not distinguish between wolves and other animals. Any creature unfortunate enough to step on one was trapped, maimed, and often left to starve to death. Coyotes, foxes, bears, mountain lions, **wolverines**, European lynx, humans, and dogs have all been caught in these traps. Leg-hold traps are now illegal in Europe, but they are still used elsewhere.

Poisoned and pursued

Poisoned carcasses have also been used to kill wolves. Poisoned carcasses also kill many natural scavengers, such as bears, coyotes, foxes, wolverines, jackals, vultures, ravens, and crows. In 1909 the state of Montana even tried a kind of biological control, ordering its vets to capture wolves and infect them with **mange,** so that it would spread to other wolves. This was an incredibly reckless policy because mange can also infect other game **species,** domestic livestock, and dogs. In some places dogs have been used to pursue and corner wolves and other **predators,** which are then shot.   Today, wolves are pursued across open country in planes or helicopters and shot from the air. In

A government worker in Minnesota sets a trap for catching wolves. He is putting it close to a cow carcass that has been laid out as bait.

parts of the Russian **tundra**, hunting from airplanes has driven the tundra wolf into the forest, where it has bred with another **subspecies**, the Eurasian wolf.

Aftereffects

When wolves are removed from an area, their former prey—deer—usually multiplies until it outgrows the local food supply. Then, in a hard winter, the animals starve to death in great numbers. The local vegetation is destroyed by overgrazing and may take years to grow back. This removes a food supply for rodents and many other small mammals and birds that feed on plants or their seeds. If wolves are not removed from an area, there is much less of a fluctuation in the population. In places where the wolf has been removed, other predators increase unless they, too, are killed by poison or traps laid for the wolves. But without the wolf leftovers, scavenging animals are deprived of easy meals.

A wolf scientist

In 1939 Adolph Murie conducted the first scientific study of wolves. He was employed to help the Mount McKinley Park Service in Alaska plan the wolves' future management. He investigated the relationship between wolves and their prey (mostly mountain sheep and caribou). To most people's surprise, he discovered that wolves and prey are usually in balance, and that wolves prey mainly on sick, old, and very young animals. By removing the sick they help maintain the health of the prey population, and they also prevent it outgrowing its food supply. This means that the prey does not suffer mass starvation and dramatic falls in population. This was the start of a big change in public opinion about the wolf in North America.

The Wolves of Isle Royale

Isle Royale is an island in Lake Superior. In 1949, during a severe winter, an ice bridge to the mainland formed and a pair of unrelated wolves from Ontario crossed it. They found lots of moose and no humans, and began to breed there. In 1958 Durward Allen began a study of these wolves, and his young Ph.D. student, David Mech, took it up in 1959. The study continues to this day, with the aid of volunteers from all over the world.

Wolves track a moose across a snowy landscape on Isle Royale on the United States/Canadian border. Surveys from the air are important in assessing the numbers of wolves and their prey.

A good influence?

Until the wolves arrived, the moose population on Isle Royale had followed the pattern of extreme fluctuation—first becoming too numerous, then overgrazing and dying of malnutrition. With the arrival of the wolves, the population stabilized, and fluctuations became less extreme. Many moose produced twins and their reproduction rates rose, so they were obviously very healthy. This demonstrated that **predator** and prey are more or less in balance in the long term—and that the presence of wolves does not necessarily reduce the numbers of moose and other prey. This discovery had a great influence on public attitudes to the wolf and helped persuade the government to reduce its slaughter.

At first David Mech found that the wolves killed mainly the very young, old, or diseased moose. But in the 1970s they began to take moose of prime breeding age. Coping with the deep snow of a severe winter had weakened the moose. By 1980, after three harsh winters, there were 50 wolves in several packs—one wolf every 3 square miles (8 square kilometers), twice the highest wolf density ever recorded. As a result, the moose population fell dramatically.

A new puzzle

In the early 1980s many of the wolves caught **canine parvovirus** from dogs taken illegally to the island.

By 1982 only 15 wolves survived. In 1988, the wolf population on Isle Royale fell again, and by 1993 there were only 12 left. No pups were born for several years, despite the highest-ever density of moose. As the moose population increased to 2,400 animals in 1995, there were still only 15 wolves on the island.

For a decade after the virus was eliminated, the wolves did not recover. A cause for this may have been lack of diversity. If animals (including humans) repeatedly breed with close relatives, they become less fertile, have less resistance to disease, and suffer high infant mortality. Scientists feared the Isle Royale wolves might not recover, but in 1996 they began to breed again. By the year 2000 there were 29. Clearly, there is still much to learn about the interactions between wolves and their environment.

The Magic Pack moves in

In November 1985 a very special event took place. A pack of 12 wolves, the Magic Pack (so named because it has a tendency to disappear for long periods and then suddenly reappear), crossed the border from British Columbia in Canada, where wolves are protected, into Montana's Glacier National Park. The following spring they produced the first pups to be born in the western United States for more than 50 years. Since then, their descendants have multiplied and formed several packs. Although the pack's increase has coincided with an upsurge of public sympathy towards the wolf, many of these wolves have been shot, trapped, or poisoned.

The world famous wolf expert David Mech carries a drugged wolf back to camp, where scientists will measure it and investigate its state of health.

31

Captive Wolves

Many **endangered species** have been saved by captive breeding. This involves raising the animals in captivity. If captive populations become large enough, attempts may be made to reintroduce some of the animals into the wild where large enough areas of suitable **habitat** remain. Wolves are not easy to keep in captivity. Ideally they need a large area in which to roam. Unrelated wolves that are forced together can go through a stressful and violent struggle to sort out their dominance relationships.

On the brink of extinction

In 1967 the red wolf was declared an endangered species. By the 1970s it was almost **extinct** in the wild. Unable to find mates of their own species, many red wolves had taken to mating with coyotes, and pure-blooded red wolves were disappearing. Only a few remained in Texas and Louisiana. The United States Fish and Wildlife Service found only 14 pure-blooded red wolves among the 400 remaining animals, and between 1974 and 1979 these were sent to a breeding center in the state of Washington. Some of the offspring of the 14 red wolves that bred were taken to other breeding centers across the country.

Collars emitting radio signals were fastened onto the wolves to track them upon their reintroduction into the wild. Captive-bred red wolves were released onto Bulls Island off the coast of South Carolina, where human contact was reduced to a minimum. For the first few months, carcasses were left for them to ensure they had enough food. Would they still have the necessary hunting and survival skills?

Animal handler Don Bailey socializes with two captive gray wolves at a wolf park in Indiana. Such parks are used to breed wolves in the hope of introducing them to the wilderness areas that have lost their wolf populations.

This red wolf lives at the International Wolf Center in Minnesota. Captive breeding and reintroduction into wilderness areas is helping to save the endangered red wolf.

Success stories

The wolves did well, and in 1987 the first pair was released at the Alligator River National Wildlife Refuge in North Carolina. By 1993 some 30 red wolves were breeding there. In 1991 more were released in the Great Smoky Mountains National Park in Tennessee, and other reserves. By 2003 more than 280 pups had been born in the wild—for the time being, the red wolf was out of danger.

The Mexican wolf, the smallest North American wolf **subspecies** that once roamed the oak woodlands of Arizona, New Mexico, Texas, and Mexico, appears to be extinct in the wild. In 1980 the last 5 individuals were caught to start a captive breeding program. Since 1998 small numbers of captive-bred Mexican wolves have been released in Arizona and New Mexico. By late 2002, there were 28 wolves in the wild in 8 packs.

Wolf-dog hybrids

Wolf lovers and people wanting a status symbol are often tempted to keep wolves or wolf-dog **hybrids** as pets. Many of these animals are later abandoned to wolf refuges. It took thousands of years to breed the domestic dog species from the wild wolf, and evolution cannot be repeated in a few months. Any wolf-dog mix may be more wolf-like than dog-like. Most so-called wolf attacks on humans are made by wolf-dog hybrids. Domesticated wolves lose their fear of humans, but keep their natural instincts to chase prey that runs. Dogs, cats, and small children may trigger this instinct, with deadly consequences. Wolves do not make good guard dogs either. They are naturally afraid of the unfamiliar and will hide from visitors, rather than bark at them.

The Yellowstone Wolves

This wolf has been caught in a net fired from a helicopter in Yellowstone National Park. It will be fitted with a radio collar, so that its movements can be tracked, then it will be re-released.

Now that public opinion is turning in favor of the wolf, attempts are being made to return it to some of its former homes. The most obvious problems arising from this are the wolf's tendency to kill livestock, its effect on the livelihoods of local farmers, and opposition from hunters. In 1982 the United States government amended the **Endangered Species** Act to allow reintroduced wolves to be designated as experimental rather than endangered. This permits **ranchers** to kill problem animals that threaten human life or wipe out livestock on their own land, and also provides for permits to reduce wolves in similar circumstances on public lands. When necessary, problem wolves may be trapped and moved to other areas.

One of the earliest reintroductions was at Yellowstone National Park. Yellowstone is a large area of mountains, forests, grasslands, and lakes. Wolves were deliberately eliminated from the park in the 1920s to protect the large herds of elk and other plant eaters. The elk then thrived to the point where they were destroying large areas of vegetation.

After 20 years of heated public consultation, campaigns by wolf support groups, and various legal actions, 31 gray wolves from Canada were released into Yellowstone in 1996. The wolves were first held in prerelease pens, where it was hoped they would bond and form packs (lone wolves are more likely to wander far from the release site). Each wolf released was fitted with a radio collar and its movements were tracked.

By early 2002, Yellowstone and the surrounding area had 250 wolves in 28 packs. However, by then the wolves had killed some 97 cattle and 426 sheep, and 59 wolves had been destroyed because they repeatedly preyed on livestock. This was actually far fewer than had been predicted. Nevertheless, there is still hostility toward the wolves from local ranchers.

At Yellowstone, the group Defenders of Wildlife funded a compensation plan for ranchers. While compensation plans help reduce hostility, claims can be hard to prove. Wolves quickly eat their kills, and also eat animals that have died from other causes. Of the $12 million already spent by Operation Wolfstock to return wolves to Yellowstone and also to central Idaho, a significant proportion is made up of compensation claims and legal fees.

Visitors enjoy the public wolf howls at the International Wolf Center in Minnesota. If they are lucky, the center's resident wolves will howl back.

Ecotourism

Without public support, wolf recovery programs will fail. One of the best ways to win over the public is to give people the opportunity to see wolves. **Ecotourism**— where tourists visit places to see wildlife—is promoted by wolf refuges, where displaced wild wolves or unwanted pets end up, and by parks and reserves where wolves have been reintroduced. Public howls are popular—experienced staff mimic wolf howls, and the real wolves howl back. Exhibitions, TV programs, talks, wolf information and activity centers, wolf watching vacations, and wolf merchandise all help to improve the wolf's image. They also raise money for **conservation** and provide jobs and income for the local community.

Keeping Track of Wolves

Working with wolves is an exhausting job. It can consist of long wilderness hikes, carrying camping gear and bags full of deer bones. Studying wolf behavior involves spending long periods with a particular wolf pack in an area close to the breeding den or rest area. It can mean watching wolves at a distance with a powerful telescope or binoculars, and following them on foot. Wolves leave very distinctive footprints on the ground and in snow.

Scientists study the relationships between wolves and their prey (including livestock) to judge the impact of wolves in a particular area. Wolf territories can cover hundreds of square miles, so scientists often survey the area by plane or helicopter (by plane is quieter) to locate the pack.

Radios for wolves

Wolves are often fitted with radio collars transmitting signals that can be picked up by a handheld radio receiver. The wolves are first trapped, either by shooting tranquilizing darts into them (often done from low-flying planes), or by driving them into nets (this is more distressing for the wolves). Some radio collars transmit signals to satellites orbiting Earth, so scientists can follow the wolves' movements on a computer. Scientists may also inject a chemical into a wolf that will show up in its droppings for some time afterward. Analysis of wolf droppings shows the kinds of food a wolf has eaten and any diseases it might have. The droppings help scientists discover which individuals are killing livestock.

A wolf is fitted with a radio collar.

▶

The radio signals emitted by the collar can be picked up by a handheld antenna, so scientists can tell where a wolf is without having to follow it on the ground.

If the scientists get the chance to follow the pack, they record the frequency with which the wolves attack, how often they succeed in killing their prey, and the age and sex of the prey. A lot can be learned without ever seeing a wolf. Scientists look for the remains of animals killed by wolves. Any kills seen from the air are later investigated on the ground. Blood on the ground or snow, tracks relating to a chase, or signs of a struggle may all suggest a wolf attack.

Reading the past

From the animal tracks and remains, the scientists can find out information about the prey population. The information is put together to get a complete record of wolf and prey numbers, movements, and kills.

Old bones

Once they find a kill, the scientists remove bones for measuring later. The lower jaws and teeth provide clues to the prey's age at death, and the leg bones, hips, and back can be checked for **arthritis** and other diseases. The bone marrow indicates how fit the prey was, and the skull size (brain volume) provides clues to how the animal was affected by nutrition early in life.

Saving European and Russian Wolves

The **tundra,** northern forests, and grassy plains of Russia and its neighboring countries are so large that many wolves still live there. In Russia, Mongolia, and China, hunters trap thousands every year for their fur, and there is also some trapping in parts of Canada, where the fur is used mainly to trim parkas. No one knows how many wolves remain in the wilderness areas of China, Mongolia, and Central Asia. Even here, wolves are losing their prey to human hunters. In just 10 years, 90 percent of the **saiga antelopes** of the Central Asian **steppes** have been killed for their horns, which are used in eastern medicine. The loss of such an important prey means that wolves are more likely to kill livestock, or enter urban areas to feed on garbage.

The Downtown Pack

In the Carpathian Mountains of Romania, a radio-collared wolf pack, nicknamed the Downtown Pack, scavenges in the town of Brasov at night, and calmly walks back out of town during the morning rush hour. In Eastern Europe, wolves scavenging in cities interbreed with local stray dogs. The **hybrid** offspring are aggressive and dangerous. If human campers and hikers leave food lying around, this leads to more unwelcome encounters with wolves. There have been some attacks on people, especially children.

A pack of wolves howls in a German forest. Howling is a good way to communicate over long distances, in dense forest, or at night. Each wolf has a different howl.

An Irish wolfhound, once called a wolfdog, is the tallest breed of dog. It was bred almost 2,000 years ago to hunt wolves and elk, and accompanied Irish nobles to war.

People out, wolves in

Europe's wolves have survived in remote areas, especially in mountains and forests. In many parts of Europe, sheep, goats, and cattle tend to be kept in fields or mountain meadows rather than (as in North America) on large areas of grassland that are hard to patrol. Since the 1950s Europeans have abandoned their small farms in the mountains and rural areas for the towns. This decrease in the number of farmers has reduced the conflict with wolves.

Europeans have become more enthusiastic about nature and **conservation**—and the wolf—than they used to be. European laws protect the wolf as an **endangered species.** In 1989 the World Wildlife Fund (WWF) set up the Large **Carnivore** Initiative for Europe (LCIE) to explore people's attitudes about large carnivores, such as wolves, lynx, **wolverines,** and bears.

The Irish wolfhound

In the 1600s Ireland had so many wolves it was called Wolfland. The bounty for killing a wolf was $10—a lot of money in those days. Wolf hunting was a popular sport among the nobility, who used a special kind of greyhound— the Irish wolfhound—to outrun and kill wolves. The earliest record of an Irish wolfhound dates from Roman times, in 391 C.E. The wolfhound is the tallest breed of dog, measuring 31 inches (81 centimeters) at the shoulder. It has good eyesight and great strength.

Wolves are moving back to many of the areas from which they were once eliminated. They are moving back into Norway and Sweden from Finland. Since gaining partial protection in 1971, Italian wolf numbers are rising, and wolves have spread across the border into France, the Alps (including the Mercantour National Park), and into Switzerland and the Pyrenees. Wolves have been increasing in Poland since the 1950s and are moving out into adjacent countries. With wolves making a comeback in Europe on their own, there are no major plans for reintroductions.

The Future of the Gray Wolf

Wolves need a huge area of unspoiled wilderness in which to find enough prey. Russia and Canada still have plenty of suitable **habitats** left, but elsewhere some wolf **subspecies** (for example, the red wolf and Mexican wolf) are dying out. Even in countries with large wilderness areas, wolf prey is often hunted almost to **extinction,** and wolves are driven to prey on livestock, or supplement their diet with garbage. Captive breeding and reintroduction programs only work if there are suitable areas with enough prey for wolves released into the wild.

The Mexican wolf (shown above in a reserve) is a small subspecies of gray wolf. It probably became extinct in the wild around 1980, but was saved by captive breeding, though numbers are still very small.

It is important for the public to be on the side of the wolf for programs like this to work. Television programs and the excellent coverage provided by many nature magazines have all helped. Wolf refuges, where people can join in public howls or see wolves and hear talks about them, also boost public awareness of wolves and their needs.

Keeping the wolves out

Even today, wherever wolves are making a comeback, there is conflict with farmers. French farmers are not at all pleased with the recent arrivals from Italy. Although the government compensates the farmer for the loss of his or her sheep, there is the inconvenience of having to buy more stock. Losses are more of a problem today because farming practices have changed. In the past shepherds and their dogs stayed with their sheep and goats on the hills, bringing them into safer pens closer to the farmhouse at night. In many parts of Europe today livestock are left in the fields alone and unprotected. In Spain, loss of sheep to wolves is ten times higher in the mountains, where livestock is left to roam, than in the valleys, where they are brought into enclosures at night. Farmers need very strong, high fences to keep out determined wolves, although electric fencing has proved helpful.

Guard dogs

In some mountainous parts of Europe, dogs are used to guard sheep and goats. When wolves meet dogs, they usually do not try to attack them, and can even greet them like other wolves. As puppies, sheep-guarding dogs are raised with lambs, and form social bonds with the sheep. They are trained not to attack livestock, but to protect the animals from **predators.**

In some parts of Europe, shepherds have bred special dogs to guard their sheep. In the Pyrenees, small dogs called Labrits herd the sheep into a corner of a valley at night, where large Pyrenean mountain dogs keep watch for wolves. Long ago these guard dogs were fitted with wide collars covered in sharp spikes, and in areas where bears were a threat, they might even have had spike-covered body armor. In some places, shepherds used to walk on stilts so that they could spot wolves approaching in the distance. Today in Italy, the WWF is training a traditional sheep-guarding breed, the Abruzzo mastiff, and supplying these dogs to farmers.

A dog guards a flock of sheep in the Tolfa mountains in Italy. Such dogs have been bred and specially trained to defend the flock against attack by wolves.

How Can You Help?

It is surprising how much just one person can do to help a threatened **species.** Many rescue plans have succeeded because of the inspiration and determination of one person. One of the most important things you can do to help the wolf is to spread the word about its needs, and let people know about some misguided ideas they may have about it.

You can become well informed by reading books about wolves and by looking at websites about them on the Internet. See if your local **conservation** group offers talks about wolves. If it does not, suggest it provide some.

Adopt a wolf

Several wolf organizations have programs where you can adopt a wolf. You pay a regular small amount of money that helps the organization's work, and in return you receive pictures and information about a particular wolf in their care—your wolf. You may even get the chance to meet your wolf.

If you are lucky enough to have a wolf refuge or zoo near you (or can visit one on vacation), go to see wolves for yourself. Look at their fur and admire the many different shades of color in it. Gaze at those wonderful golden eyes. Watch how effortlessly wolves move. Listen for the different kinds of wolf conversation noises. Join in a public howl. Visit the information center to see what you can find out about them.

*MacKenzie was the **alpha** female of the Ambassador Pack at Minnesota's International Wolf Center until her eyesight began to fail with age. She belongs to the Great Plains wolf **subspecies,** and is a darker color than most gray wolves.*

Check out the websites of the numerous wolf refuges and wolf conservation charities. Some have free newsletters to keep you up to date with all their latest activities, including how newly reintroduced wolf packs are doing.

Wolf shopping

Wolf organizations often sell fun gifts with pictures of wolves— paperweights, trinkets, T-shirts, postcards, and posters. There are also videos and DVDs of wolves, as well as CDs of wolf sounds.

You may wish to try and organize a fundraiser to help raise money for wolf organizations. Remember, every little bit helps.

Wolves on the Internet

There are many Internet sites on wolves. Try searching with wolf or wolves and words like conservation, reintroduction, refuge, rescue center, and so on. Some wolf conservation groups have regular e-newsletters. Others keep online diaries about wolves they are caring for or about packs that have been reintroduced to new areas.

Wolf adoption kits include specific information about the wolf you have chosen.

Glossary

adapt   alter behavior or structure to cope with changing circumstances, such as the environment or weather or availability of particular types of prey

alpha   refers to the dominant pair (having the highest rank) of wolves in a pack, called the alpha male and alpha female

arthritis   inflammation of the joints

canine parvovirus   highly contagious disease of dogs and their relatives that causes loss of energy and appetite, diarrhea, vomiting, and sometimes death

carnivore   meat-eating animal

cattle drive   long-distance movement of cattle, guided and driven on by people on horseback

conservation   management of wild animals, plants, and other natural resources to ensure their survival in the future

distemper   highly contagious viral disease of certain mammals

ecotourism   tourism for people interested in wild parts of the world

endangered   in serious danger of becoming extinct

extinct   no longer existing

flank   fleshy part of side of the body between the ribs and the hip

fluke   wormlike animal that lives as a parasite on other animals

gangrene   rotting and death of animal tissues caused by loss of blood supply as a result of injury or infection

genus   group of closely related species

habitat   place where a particular organism lives

hookworm   small blood-sucking worm that lives as a parasite in the intestines of other animals

hybrid   organism that is the offspring of two different (but usually closely related) species that have bred together

legislation   law

mange   contagious skin disease of animals, caused by mites

migrant   person who moves from one place to another

migrate   move from one place to another

nomad person who moves from place to place to find pasture and food

Nordic of, or relating to, Scandinavia

prairie extensive stretch of level or rolling uncultivated grassland in North America

predator animal that hunts and kills other animals (prey) to eat

rabid suffering from rabies

rancher someone who owns or works on a ranch—a large farm where livestock are reared

rut energetic courtship rituals and fights between deer

saiga antelope pale-colored hoofed mammal about 30 inches (76 centimeters) tall at the shoulder that lives on the steppe grasslands of eastern Europe, Russia, and Asia

species scientific name for a particular kind of plant, animal, or other living thing. Two individuals of the same species can reproduce and have babies. Individuals from separate species cannot.

steppe large stretch of level, treeless grassland found in the drier parts of southeastern Europe, Russia, and Asia

subspecies population of animals or other living things that differs slightly from others of the same species. Subspecies are usually restricted to a particular geographical area.

tundra type of vegetation found in high latitudes and on high mountain tops that consist of low-growing shrubby plants, grasses, sedges, rushes, mosses, and lichens, but no trees

wolverine powerfully built member of the weasel family that looks like a small bear

Useful Contacts and Further Reading

Conservation groups

Defenders of Wildlife
1244 19th Street NW
Washington, DC 20036

Isle Royale Wolf-Moose Study
Michigan Tech Fund/Alumni House
Michigan Technical University
Houghton, MI 49931

Mexican Wolf Coalition of New Mexico
7239 Isleta Boulevard SW
Albuquerque, NM 87105

Mission: Wolf
P.O. Box 211
Silver Cliff, CO 81249

National Wildlife Federation
11100 Wildlife Center Drive
Reston, VA 20190-5362

The International Wolf Center
1396 Highway 169
Ely, MN 55731

The Red Wolf Fund
Tacoma Zoological Society
5400 North Pearl Street
Tacoma, WA 98407

Wolf!
Box 29
Lafayette, IN 47902

Wolf Ecology Project
School of Forestry
University of Montana
Missoula, MT 59812

Wolf Education Fund
Zion Natural History Association
Springdale, UT 84767

Wolf Haven International
3111 Offut Lake Road
Tenino, WA 98589

Books

Busch, Robert H. *The Wolf Almanac: A Celebration of Wolves and Their World.* Allston, Mass.: Fitzhenry & Whiteside, 1998.

Busch, Robert H., ed. *Wolf Songs: The Classic Collection of Writings About Wolves.* San Francisco: Sierra Club Books, 1997.

Hall, Elizabeth. *Child of the Wolves.* Minneapolis: Sagebrush Education Resources, 1997.

Lopez, Barry Holstun. *Of Wolves and Men.* Minneapolis: Sagebrush Education Resources, 1995.

McIntyre, Rick. *A Society of Wolves: National Parks and the Battle over the Wolf.* Stillwater, Minn.: Voyageur Press, 1996.

Mowat, Farley. *Never Cry Wolf: Amazing True Story of Life among Arctic Wolves.* Minneapolis: Sagebrush Education Resources, 2001.

Scholl, Elizabeth. *Wolves.* San Diego: Kidhaven, 2003.

Solway, Andrew. *Wolves and Other Dogs.* Chicago: Heinemann Library, 2004.

Spilsbury, Louise and Richard Spilsbury. *A Pack of Wolves.* Chicago: Heinemann Library, 2003.

Index